Life Is A Party

That Comes With Exams

A Youth Empowerment Guide

Denise Crittendon

Healing Pathways...For A New Generation

Life Is A Party That Comes With Exams

By Denise Crittendon
Published by Esteem Multi Media
200 Riverfront Drive, #8j
Detroit, MI 48226

www.esteemmultimedia.com
Dcrittendon@esteemmultimedia.com

Photography: Clarence Tabb

Cover Design and layout: William Townley of Tvisuals

ISBN   978-0-615-23407-6

Library of Congress Catalog Card Number in publication data.

Printed in the United States of America

In loving memory of my niece,
Rhonda Crittendon,
a remarkable young woman of principle,
grace, peace and true inner beauty.

Acknowledgments

Thank you to teen models, Priscilla Garza, Matt Smith, Briana Jefferson, Jasmine Nye, Breanne Mikus, Torri Smith, Zack Danielson, James Smith Moore and Breana Cage. A special thank you to Edna Williams of Oak Park Youth Assistance, Karla Hall of DTE Energy, Loretta Smith of Comerica Inc. and to Diana Jones, formerly of Blue Cross Blue Shield of Michigan.

Here's a shout out to students who previewed the book: Yemisi Odetoyinbo and Marquise Tillerson. And kudos to Lynette Wall for photo assistance and Sonya Vann for proofreading. Also, a special, heart-felt appreciation goes out to Janice Joseph, Sharon James, Janice Hayes Kyser, Kat Lawshea, Diane Smith, Vivian Sanders, William Townley, Pastor Patrick Gahagen, Ernestyne Tuck, Ruthie Gordon, Mary Lanier, Chichita Young, Fannie McGruder, Geraldine Edwards, Madeline Edwards, Paula Edwards, Diane Edwards, The Rev. Pat McCaughan, the Women's Club of Immanuel Lutheran Church in Detroit, the Harbin family and all of the incredible friends who served as angels during the hour of my deepest need. Thank You for showing me how to pick up the torch and carry on the legacy of my mother, Nellie Crittendon.

CONTENTS

"The audacity of hope! In the end, that is God's greatest gift to us, the bedrock of this nation. A belief in things not seen. A belief that there are better days ahead."

-President Barack Obama

LET'S GET THIS PARTY STARTED

Hey You!
Bet you never thought life was a party. How could it be? People are always telling you what to do and what not to do, especially when you're having fun. Teachers and parents talk about going to school and studying. Or they tell you to get off the phone, not to stay up late or out too late.

That's not a party! That's boredom! And when a real party does happen, you don't always get to go, do you? Either you're on a punishment, or you don't have a ride or someone will tell you *no*, just to be mean.

Just like that, you're cut off from the action. So how can anyone describe life as a party? How can this book convince you that all of "Life Is A Party That Comes With Exams?" The whole experience seems like an exam sometimes, and you're sick of it.

Well, that's part of the problem. You might need to learn how to separate exam time from party time. Maybe you need to figure out how to take the tests and get them over with so you can have more fun.

You see, that's how life works, sort of like school. There's a world of opportunities, adventures and excitement awaiting you. But you don't get to enjoy them if you're still back in class, sulking about a problem that happened a long time ago. It's kind of like getting a note to take home or being sent to detention. If you don't do it and get it over with, you get in more and more trouble. But if you deal with it and get it out of the way, you can move on.

1

Video games are a good example of this. They're fun. They're thrilling. But, if you're always losing, does that mean the video game is lousy or does that mean you need to become a better player?

And so it is with the party of life. It's going on all around you all the time but if you have a chip on your shoulder, you're missing out. If you're not doing what you're supposed to do, you're getting left behind. And if you're walking around thinking that the world revolves around you then no one is going to take you seriously. In other words, you're not improving your game. You're still taking the test.

Does that sound like you or someone you know?

Be patient. Within the pages of this book, you're going to find out what you probably always suspected – life can be fun. No, it might not always seem like it. There's trouble lurking when you don't expect it. You never know when you're going to be hit with bad grades, relationships that don't work out or friends who gossip and act phony.

Nothing messes up a good time more than people who give other people a hard time. But, listen to this: When things are going wrong, when everything is falling apart at home, even when you have an attitude about something, you can keep the party of your life going. How? Turn the page and find out.

Love, Peace and Lots of Joy,

Denise Crittendon

CHAPTER ONE
THE MUSIC IN YOUR MIND

L isten.

Can you hear that sound? It's the rhythm of your own emotions. Be still and check it out. Do you hear it now? It's fast, it's furious, it's happy, it's sad. It's slow when you are not feeling well and quick when you're in a good mood.

It is the music in your mind.

Whatever you are feeling at the moment is like a string of musical notes rippling inside of you. It's the part of your personality that makes you unique.

What does your music sound like? Get quiet again and tune in to it. Is it steady like Chris Brown's "Run It" or mellow like Mariah Carey singing "E=MC2"?

Is it bouncy like Hannah Montana, smooth like Justin Timberlake or aggressive like Jay-Z? Is your music positive or is your music negative?

Listen one last time. Now, block out the sound of your favorite tune, grow silent and pay attention to your own voice. Hear the rumblings of your anger or the thunder of your joy?

Your thoughts have a beat, a steady rat-a-tat-tat that is separate from the music you hear on the radio. Your thoughts have their own style. They are a mix of feelings and each one is as original as you are.

That's because your thoughts are your own personal form of harmony. They are like a marching band thumping around inside your mind daily. You hear them all the time.

"I'm buying some shoes like that tomorrow. Those are bad."

"I'm tired of wearing this."

"This is alright."

"I'm bored."

"I know that girl doesn't think I'm going to do that."

"I mean, it's like he thinks he's the only boy at school."

"We're getting homework. Again!!!"

Thoughts rattle on and on all day. In a 24-hour period, you'll probably have about 40,000 to 50,000 of them. But you're the only one who hears the ongoing complaining or the excitement, the joy or the pain. You're the only one who knows what's up in your mind.

And you are the only one who can give meaning to your private music. That's what poets, musicians and rap stars do. They pay close attention to the whispers in their heads and decide to give them center stage in their lives.

A Rapper's Emotion

A rapper, for instance, takes his or her feelings about a situation and combines them with a tune. But it's not just any tune. Most rappers play around with the drama in their minds. When they're upset, they might hear a strong, banging noise. When they're pleased, they probably hear a beat inside their heads that makes them feel like dancing. All they have to do to get their groove on is come up with some powerful words and before you know it, they have a new CD.

Entertainers have a knack for recognizing their feelings and using those feelings to communicate with the rest of us. They know that the ideas whipping through their brains are a source of power.

That's because thoughts are power. Thoughts are an important part of a person's identity and the key to changing their lives.

Think about it. When you're on the dance floor, it's almost as if your thoughts are sizzling. When you're having fun, laughing and kicking it with friends, it's like you're flying high.

When you're down and out, it's the other way around. Someone has just yelled at you or you're having an argument. Your heartbeat speeds up and suddenly your thoughts feel heavy. You might even walk around that way for a while. You frown, get an attitude and try to bring everyone else around you down.

Take Your Power Back!

Like most people, you are acting that way because you have been taught that circumstances have control over what you think and feel. You really believe that if things are going wrong, you have a right to blame others or hold a grudge. In some cases, you might even resort to hitting, fighting or calling people names.

But what if someone told you that you can remain positive when everyone else seems negative? What if someone said you don't have to feel sad every time something you don't like happens? What if someone suggested that your life will improve if you change the way you react to problems?

Well, you probably wouldn't believe them. After all, it doesn't make sense to be happy when nothing's going right. Does it? Let's say you get into a fight with a friend or your parents do something that ticks you off. Of course you're upset. Most people would be. But you don't have to stay that way. You have a couple of choices. You can rant and rave and get depressed. Or you can take your power back.

Taking your power back is easy. You simply grab control of what you are thinking. Thoughts, ideas and emotions come and go. It's up to you which ones get to live on in your mind and which ones get kicked to the curb. It's up to you who owns the power. You? Or the person who made you mad? You? Or the person who tried to make you feel you're not smart or that you don't look good?

If someone says something unkind or rejects you in any way, the music in your mind pounds like hundreds of loud drums. But when you refuse to listen to the noise, you get to run the show. You do that by flooding your mind with positive music. Rather than focus on the bad stuff, you can deliberately think about something funny a friend once said. Or you can remember a time you said something that made everyone laugh.

That's called hammering in new thoughts. A philosopher named Emmet Fox once described an old thought as a rusty nail in a sturdy piece of wood. If a carpenter wants to get rid of the old nail, he holds a new nail directly behind the old one. Then, he takes a hammer and hammers the new nail right through. As the new nail is pushed in, the old nail is pushed out.

And so it is with old, dead, rotting thoughts. Shove them out! Got doubts? Replace them with confidence. Get an attitude that sparkles, shimmers and shines. You see, no one thinks inside of your mind but you. And you have the power to think anything you want. So why waste time thinking: *"I'm too fat." "I'm too skinny," "I'm too tall." "I'm too short" "I'm not a good athlete. " "I don't like my hair." "I'm furious." "I don't get mad, I get even." "I'm not a good student." "No one understands."*

Try this instead: *"I'm fine just the way I am." "I like myself just the way I am and I'm getting better all the time." "I am a good student." "This haircut looks great on me." "I am in control of my temper." "I am peaceful, and I am calm." "I don't hold on to anger. It's not worth it." "I have the kind of face that goes with any hairstyle." "The experiences in my life are preparing me for something wonderful."*

You can think whatever you want in the private space of your mind. So pick out some lyrics that you enjoy hearing. Remember, the beats pumping in your head are your own personal language. When they're angry, you're giving your power away. When they're filled with resentment and jealously, you're giving power away.

Take it back! Sweep out your brain. Start telling yourself you look good, you're smart and you can accomplish your goals. Tell yourself you are in control of you. No one tells you who you are because you already know you are incredible. Tell yourself that no one is invading this space inside of you. This is your kingdom, your castle. You and only you decide what kinds of thoughts sneak in.

This might come as a surprise, but NBA star Michael Jordan wasn't always tall and he wasn't always an excellent athlete. But he was someone who refused to allow others to tell him what he could or couldn't achieve. He made up his mind at an early age that he was going to succeed. So he practiced, practiced, practiced. In addition, he knew how to handle his thoughts. Every day, he told himself that he was a great basketball player. He imagined himself flying in the air, slam-dunking the ball. He held on to that scene in his mind and pictured it daily. Then, he would think about it, think about it and think about it.

When you think about something long enough and hard enough, you believe it. So what are you thinking right now? It's important to ask yourself that every once in a while. Stop and notice how you are feeling. Then, put it into words.

If you don't like what you're thinking, there's one thing you, and only you, can do with those ideas floating around inside your brain.

Change Them!

Music Exercises

1. Many songwriters and rappers pay attention to what they are thinking and write it down. If it isn't what they had in mind, they come up with something better. They replace the ideas they don't want with ideas that give them a feeling of pride and power. You can do the same thing but in a different way. Draw a line down the center of the page. On one side, write the word NEGATIVE. Beneath it, write down things you think that you probably shouldn't be thinking. On the other side, write the word POSITIVE, then list all the positive ideas that enter your mind.

2. Look at your list of thoughts and pretend they are a song set to music. If this doesn't come easy, keep trying to pretend. What kind of music would the negative thoughts have? How about the positive thoughts? What do you think that music would sound like? See if you can turn the ideas you wrote in the positive column into a rap song. Make them rhyme.

3.What do you think about most? Is it something positive? Write a few sentences about what's on your mind most of the time. It doesn't matter what it is. It could be a girlfriend or boyfriend. Share your thoughts.

CHAPTER TWO
DANCE TO YOUR OWN BEAT

Quick, what's your favorite dance?
Do you enjoy moving freestyle? Or would you rather take it slow? Whatever you like, when the music is pumping and the party is packed, there's only one thing that really matters: *that you dance to your own beat.*

That means not listening to what someone else has to say about what you should be doing on the dance floor and not worrying about what anyone thinks. If you're too busy concentrating on who's watching you, you're not going to enjoy yourself very much. And if someone tried to interrupt you and tell you how to move, that person wouldn't remain on your list of friends for long.

The bottom line is that everyone has his or her own form of self-expression. It's reflected in the way they dress, the way they talk and even the way they dance. It's a personal thing and most of us wouldn't appreciate a lot of criticism and unnecessary direction.

But what about everyday life? Has anyone ever said you weren't cool or called you a baby just because you weren't interested in doing something they wanted to do? Well, your friends wouldn't stop you while you were dancing to tell you how to move your body. Likewise, they shouldn't suggest what you should do before, after or during school hours.

You have your own beat and, odds are, no one is trying to prevent you from dancing to it. Apply that same philosophy to the classroom or after school. It doesn't matter where you are or what's happening. You might be visiting friends or doing homework. However, just like you make the decision to get on the dance floor, it's up to you to make the decision how to rock and how to turn. It's up to you to say no to friends who are trying to lead you somewhere you know you shouldn't go.

If you're a good dancer, you have confidence. There's power in every step you take and you can feel it. It's in your strut, in your glide, in your stride. Your ego is soaring and you're on top of the world. Do you have that same confidence once the music stops?

You see, it's easy to feel cool when you know what you're doing and everyone seems to be on your side. It's not as easy when the mood shifts and everyone seems to want to do something that you don't feel comfortable doing. It's like they think they know more than you do. It's like they're getting all the attention. As if that isn't enough, they're trying to make you feel like a nerd just because you're using expressions like "curfew" or explaining that you have to go home.

That's when the real tests of life begin. The dance is over, but it is up to you to keep grooving to your own beat. Your own beat is the truth that pounds on and on inside of you — even after you have made the choice to do something wrong. Your own beat is the voice inside of you. It's that noise in your head that keeps haunting you. It is your conscience.

Unfortunately, it turns into a little whisper when you ignore it. For instance, if you have been taught that smoking is not a good thing or that using drugs is wrong, you have become accustomed to hearing that message. Perhaps your parents have said it. Teachers have said it. Aunts, uncles and even older brothers and sisters may have said it. You are so used to hearing that statement that it has become the law. You believe in it and you follow it. It's the only beat you know.

Then a few friends come along and try to convince you otherwise. They tell you nothing's wrong with a little weed, a little cocaine. They tell you grown-ups have gotten it all wrong. At first, you refuse to listen. Why? The message programmed inside of you is telling you just the opposite.

But your friends don't give up that easily. They keep trying. They keep teasing. They keep making sarcastic remarks. You go to parties and there they are. You go to school and they're always around. After a while, the lifelong lessons in your mind get weaker and the other voices grow as loud as a thousand drums. After a while, you give in. You start dancing to someone else's beat.

Getting Back On Beat

It's kind of confusing trying to figure out which beat is yours and which one isn't. But here are a few clues to help you get back on track:

* Find a safe spot in the neighborhood and go for a walk or a run. Or you can stay home and do sit-ups or jumping jacks. The physical activity will calm your mind and help you to think.

* Once you're ready, go talk to someone you trust. It could be a parent, but it doesn't have to be. Contact an older cousin, a young aunt, uncle or another adult who's cool. Find someone who will listen and help you sort things out.

*Maintain a journal. No one has to know about this but you. If you don't have the money for a special journal with a key, just get a notebook and hide it somewhere. Every night or a few nights a week, pull it out and write down what you are really feeling. Jot down dreams, plans and goals.

If you follow the steps above, you'll get back on beat again. If you never lost it, then these tips will help you to keep holding on. It's not always easy to stay true to who you really are — especially with so many outside influences. Just remember that just because a dream or an idea is important to you doesn't mean it is important to everyone else and vice versa. And that's perfectly okay. This is your beat we're talking about, not the rhythms and plans of your friends.

They might be good buddies. But they don't laugh like you do, walk like you do or wear their hair in the same style. You are who you are and that's okay. That's something to celebrate; not a problem that should make you feel bad. If it were, everyone in the world would look like identical twins.

That would be kind of whack, wouldn't it? What if we all had the same noses, same eyes? What if we all sounded the same whenever we spoke?

That's a strange suggestion and, yet, it's what some teens are trying to accomplish. They believe that because someone else is doing something, they should try it and they think that if someone else has a certain skill or talent, they should have that ability as well.

The reality is that every individual has his or her own gifts and qualities. We are all as precious as rare diamonds and as original as bouquets of various, hand-picked flowers. We aren't meant to be the same any more than every snowflake or every distinct drop of rain.

Did you know that every dolphin has a very unique whistle, separate from every other dolphin? And, they may look the same to us, but every zebra has a different pattern of stripes.

Nothing and no one is exact on this amazing planet we call Earth. That includes you! No one has your mannerisms, your facial expressions, your special smile. No one can do many of the things that you were born specifically to do.

Do you know anything about the late singer Selena? If you do, you're aware of the fact that she was obsessed with singing. From the time she was a young girl, all she ever wanted to do was perform on stage. Singing isn't for everyone. Not everyone has the voice to sing; the skill to be an artist or the scientific mind necessary to become a doctor. But absolutely everyone has the ability to do something.

Be honest with yourself: What do you enjoy? What activities have always come naturally to you? There is an assignment with your name on it. There is a task designed specifically for you. There is a path you are meant to walk down; there is a talent that is all yours. There is a skill you can master, a class you do well in, a job that you do best.

Yet it is up to you to determine what it is. You're not going to do it by copying the ways and habits of celebrities, acquaintances and other teens traveling down roads that lead to trouble.

Instead, get on the road that connects you to positive goals and genuine interests. Get on the road that brings out the best in you. Do the things that make you happy because they enrich your life and fill you with a sense of achievement.

Don't worry if your goals aren't flashy or don't seem to lead to fortune and fame. Be authentic. That means repairing cars or styling hair if that's what comes natural to you. That means studying computers if you like playing with video games and dabbling with high-tech gadgets. It means working in a hospital if that's what you find appealing and becoming a writer or a lawyer if you have a way with words.

Find out who you are and be that person. Look for those little things that set you apart. Find honest ways to do well and earn money. Develop those talents that have been with you since you were five or six years old.

Do not spend your life trying to be something you are not. Take your mind in another direction. Rock to your own beat. And, whatever happens, just keep on moving.

Never let anyone stop you in the middle of the dance.

Dance Exercises

1. Describe your favorite dance. Next, list your favorite songs, then describe why you like each song. Do the songs or dances capture anything about your personal attitudes or feelings about life in general? If so, jot it down.

2. Do any of the songs on your list have negative lyrics or messages? Think of some positive messages you wouldn't mind hearing instead. Write them down and repeat them to yourself daily. Say them 10 times upon rising then 10 times before going to bed.

3. Have any of your friends or acquaintances ever tried to talk you into doing something you knew you shouldn't do? What did they say and how did you respond?

4. Listen to your heart— Make a list of all the things that you truly enjoy doing. Draw five stars next to the activities you like best and one star to the one you like least. The activity with five stars is something you should consider.

CHAPTER THREE

YOUR THOUGHTS ARE LIKE DOLLAR BILLS

The sun is shining, and the sky is free of clouds. It's the perfect day to hook up with friends, go to a movie or whiz by your favorite drive-through restaurant to pick up a bite to eat.

But first you have to find transportation. Next, you better make sure you have a pocket full of cash. You'll need it to pay for the burger, to get into the theater or just to buy a bag of chips.

Just about everything has either a price tag or an admission fee. Shoes, food, homes, fast cars. None of it is free and none of it is cheap. It costs plenty of hard-earned dollars to get your hair the way you want it and your clothes right. You have to keep the cash flowing. The more you have of it, the more you can buy and the more places you can go.

Yet, there's a catch to it! It's spelled A-T-T-I-T-U-D-E. You have to have the right attitude to get a job to earn a salary to help you pay for what you need. Either that or you have to maintain a good attitude at home if you expect your parents to finance your requests.

There's more! You also have to have a winning attitude to make your life work. If you don't, all the money in the world isn't going to help you. If you're stuck with a poor attitude, you might as well be broke and homeless. A poor attitude is like a magnet that's so dull it can't even pick up paper clips. A poor attitude sucks!

Why? Attitude can be described as a series of thoughts that build upon one another and, eventually, become part of your personality. The problem is that if these thoughts are negative or angry, they don't have much power and energy. These thoughts have lost their punch and don't have the spark to attract anything good into your life.

That means that even with money, you'll find things going wrong. You can buy all the new CDs and gym shoes you want, but if you don't have decent friends you're not going to be very happy. If you're always on punishment, you're not going to feel very good. And if you're constantly getting into trouble at school, you're going to spend a lot of time in the office, collecting notes to take home.

You may have money to buy material things but you're running kind of low on mental cash. It's time for you to visit the bank inside your mind and make a deposit.

How do you make a deposit in your brain? It's easy. You start stuffing it with brand new thoughts. You see, your thoughts are like dollar bills. Whatever you think about and talk about represents what you will experience.

The "I can't" thought, for instance, is a no-no because it's a terrible investment. Every time you say "I can't," consider that you are buying that belief. If you say you can't do math, can't do well in school, can't get your game together, you are plopping several dollars onto the counter of life and making a down payment on a not-so-positive future.

Words and thoughts are so powerful that they invade your world and seriously affect the environment you live in. They are like electrical forces creating and attracting all that you think and feel. Here's one example:

Suppose your mother gave you and your brother $200 just to spend. Obviously, both of you would head straight to the mall. But what if along the way, you pass a stranger who pleads with you to purchase a huge bag of used candy wrappers and old socks. For some odd reason, you agree to the weird request. While your brother shakes his head, you give the stranger $200 for a bundle of useless rags and tattered paper. However, your brother is no fool. He continues on to the mall as planned and goes on a shopping spree. Later that night, you're mad because he's showing off his new outfits and you're stuck wearing the same old clothes. Yet, whose fault is it really? You could have shopped until you dropped. Instead, you took your money and bought garbage.

Does this story sound unbelievable? Maybe it does, but it's a perfect demonstration of what some people do every day. They walk around making negative comments about themselves and about others. They anger quickly and have a hard time getting along with others.

Not too many good things are happening in their lives and they are upset with the world. They blame their families, their classmates, the teacher, the dog, the cat. But that's not the problem.

They are the problem. Their anger is the problem. Their complaints are the problem. They make mean comments and sad statements day in and day out. They might not be aware of it, but their negative thoughts and words are responsible for their hard times. They don't realize that they have to think positive thoughts to get positive results. Instead, they're tripping. They're filling their minds with hostile ideas. As a result, life is giving them old candy wrappers and dirty socks.

Do you get the idea? They are consumed with resentment, and they keep making bad decisions. It's just like they are buying trash when they could be making a trip to the mall.

Think about that for a minute. Your mind is powerful; so how are you going to use it — for good or for bad? Are you going to use it buy what you need or to get stuck with a bag of useless junk? It's your call. Teens in messed up situations can get their lives together if they are willing to get their thoughts together.

However, there are some unfortunate circumstances involving teens who are dealing with serious drama; although they had nothing to do with making it happen. In these situations, pain and tragedy occurred when they were very young. Children born into circumstances like poverty and physical or verbal abuse at the hands of their parents are not at fault.

Of course, not everyone is facing such difficulties. But if you are, always remember to recognize yourself as a child of beauty and power. You might not be able to affect what is happening today. But, with the right focus and determination, you can affect what will happen tomorrow.

That means that you may never repair your family, but you can patch up your own thinking and take charge of your own destiny. Like everyone else, you can reach higher by stretching your imagination. If you have had a tough break, close your eyes and picture things getting better.

Never ever say, "My life is horrible," or "I hate my life." (Strike the word hate from your vocabulary now) Say to yourself: "Each and every day, my life gets better and better in every way." Repeat that even if you don't believe it. In fact, if you don't believe it, that's when you should claim it. Force yourself. Over and over again, say: "Each and every day, my life gets better and better in every way."

If you're like most people, you face both ups and downs. During the down times, think "up" thoughts. No matter who you are or what you have experienced, don't fall into the trap of constant self-pity and depression. Don't talk woe-is-me talk. Don't allow your precious thoughts to be wasted on the purchase of sticks and rocks.

Buy Positive Experiences By Making Positive Statements.

Think about pleasant dreams even when you are dealing with an unpleasant reality. Throw all the "I can't" thoughts out of your conversation. When you think of something negative, stop the idea dead in its tracks. Then, tell yourself "I am not buying that." Say "I can, I can, I can." If you have a test coming up, say "I can pass it." "I am going to pass it. I know I am." If you have doubts in your mind about anything, say "I can accomplish my goals." Say "I am powerful. I am awesome. I am strong."

There's an old R&B song that goes "Say It, Say It, Say It." Try it: Say It, Say It, then Say It again.

Remember, the clothes you buy might make you look

good on the outside. However, the knowledge and confidence you develop inside can turn your entire life around. So go ahead. DREAM BIG DREAMS! Conjure up exciting, new ideas. Tell yourself "I deserve the best, and I expect the best."

Be as powerful and as positive as you can.

Affirmation Exercises

1. Affirmations are powerful tools that can help improve your life. Repeat these statements to yourself over and over again. Start saying them in the morning, quietly to yourself or out loud. Say them several times throughout the day then again before you go to bed at night. You also can write them out on index cards and mount them on your bedroom wall or on your dresser. Keep in mind, the more you say them, the better they work. Remember this is your daily mental workout to build strong mental muscles...

Each and every day, my life gets better and better in every way.

I am attractive. I am unique. I am important.

I believe in me. I believe in my dreams.

I am powerful. I am positive. I am strong.

I am determined. I never give up.

I am peaceful, and I am calm.

I feel peace. My mind and spirit are filled with thoughts of peace.

I am always peaceful. I am a peaceful person.

I am a good student with goals and purpose.

I am enjoying a wonderful life.

I am honest. I am sincere. I am dedicated.

I am incredible. I am making my family proud.

I am an amazing person with amazing talents.

I am proud of my gifts and talents.

I am gifted and talented.

I am bursting with confidence.

I deserve the best life has to offer.

I deserve the best and I expect the best.

I am a proud, confident person.

I am strong and determined. I am achieving my goals.

I am focused and confident in all situations.

I am healthy, happy and positive.

I am a success and I am living my dreams.

I release the challenges of yesterday. I am healed and my heart is filled with self-love.

I am NOT angry about the bad times. I am grateful for the good times.

I have forgotten my disappointments. I am ready for fun and joy.

I am a magnet for positive people and positive situations.

I am honest and truthful.

I am honest. I always tell the truth.

I have let go of my disappointments. I am claiming victory.

I am precious, and I am loved.

I am powerful. I am dynamic. I am unstoppable.

I truly love and value myself.

I love myself, and I love others.

I cherish myself. I see only good.

I love myself just the way I am, and I am getting better all the time.

I am holding my head up for I am on my way up.

I totally forgive everyone, including myself.

With love in my heart, I forgive.

My heart is filled with peace, happiness and love.

2. Pick at least three affirmations and say them 25 to 30 times daily. You can say them while standing in the mirror, taking a shower or quietly to yourself throughout the day.

3. Look in the mirror, stare into your own eyes and quietly say: **"I Love You."** Try this exercise every morning.

CHAPTER FOUR

IF YOU'RE SO COOL, WHY ARE YOU PLAYING FOLLOW THE LEADER?

A grizzly wrestler with a humped back and tangled patches of hair snarls at a thin, rather pathetic looking man on the other side of the ring. But the skinny guy doesn't seem scared. It doesn't seem to matter to him that he's getting ready to fight an enemy who can't seem to stop growling. It doesn't matter that his opponent is angry and unruly. Or that he's more than three times his size. He faces him with confidence and both men prepare to swing.

But before they start, something odd happens.
The small wrestler takes one deep breath and five quick steps backwards. Then, just as his opponent approaches, he stops and stares him directly in the eye. It is an intense stare. It is strong, focused and piercing. The big guy

begins to scream. He runs in circles. He stops snarling and falls to his knees. Before long, he's flat on his stomach and the ringmaster is counting. "one, two three, four, five, six, seven, eight, nine, ten...and he's out."

The winner is a quiet, little man who didn't appear to be large enough, tough enough, mean enough to be a wrestler. The winner is a calm person who possessed something the big guy didn't seem to understand.

A powerful mind.

Okay, so it's not quite that easy. Strong minds don't win wrestling matches, strong muscles do. A mind can't be strong enough to overcome someone so large and so fierce. That's an exaggeration. Or is it?

For the next few minutes, we're going to take a look at a few things that maybe you haven't considered. They include:

* **People with strong minds have unbeatable confidence.**

* **People with unbeatable confidence believe in themselves.**

* **People who believe in themselves don't need to do what others are doing.**

* **People who don't need to do what others are doing make decisions for themselves based on what is right.**

* **People who make the right decisions for themselves are winners.**

The conclusion:
Strong minds lead to winning attitudes.

Now, back to the two guys in the ring. If Mr. Thin has a lean body but one heck of a mental attitude, he is the real winner. Mr. Snarl might have a lot of muscles but he lacks punch where it counts — in his mind.

The mind is the real leader. If you train it right, you will take the lead. Others will follow you. But you will follow no one. After all, who wants to spend their lives playing a permanent game of follow the leader? Got it?

Okay, let's move on. Now, let's say Mr. Big Muscles is so embarrassed he demands a rematch. He can't figure out what went wrong so he's determined to get back in the ring and show the timid guy whose boss.

He tries again and the same thing happens. Again. And again. And again. Finally, he's so humiliated he eases away. He goes into hiding somewhere, maybe Iceland, who knows? No one ever hears from him again.

So what just happened here? Mr. Big Stuff just doesn't have a clue. He kept focusing all of his energy on the outside (his strong arms, hands and huge chest). But he forgot to pack a heavy duty punch in his thoughts.

Here's what he should have done. He should have paid a trip to Video Game Village. Would you like to go along? Come on in. You're invited!

Welcome To Video Game Village

This is not real. This is only a video game. But the results you achieve here can last a lifetime.

This is how it works. Never mind, you know how it works. You've played video games before. Let's just do a quick run.

See those levers over there. Those are the control

pieces. Pull one and make the men in green capes fly across the screen. They are being chased by women in orange, but the faster you maneuver, the fewer points they score. Keep going faster, faster. Your men are flying. Now stop all of a sudden, quit paying attention. Look the other way. Release the lever.

They're falling now, and you're losing. The orange women are scoring points like mad because you're not actively participating. Remember, if you don't pull the lever, the men in green have no power. The power isn't with them. They are fake images on the screen. The power is in your mind. The power is in the decisions you make. The men in green have no power until you decide what to do.

The same thing applies to life. The power is not in the shoes; they are rubber and cloth. They have no control over your life, no matter what designer made them. The power is not in anything you're wearing or even the car you're driving. The power lies within you, the driver. The power is what's taking place in that space between your ears.

That's what went wrong with the grizzly wrestler. He thought his hands had the strength and that his fists packed all the punch. But the other guy was able to intimidate him just by staring him down. The other guy realized that mental strength would conquer all and it did.

He didn't need to use his hands. All he had to do was pull the right levers in his mind. But there's more. Read on.

The Brain Is Really A Computer

So you think you're smart? You think you're dumb? You think you're cute? You think you're hot? You think you're not good enough? Whatever you think, you're right.

Whether you're feeling popular or feeling sad, whether you're feeling like a failure or feeling like a success, the answer is always the same. You're right! You're right! You're right!

You see, you're the one doing the thinking. You're the one making the calls. It's up to you and only you. So, back to the original point: what do you think of yourself? Hey, you know what? You're right!

You hold the key to victory when you understand that brain power is the only power that wins in the end. But it's real important to learn how to use that key. It's also real important to understand that the brain is a computer.

It's up to you to learn how to work it. You can start by understanding that the computer is designed to imitate the brain. That means that the same approach you use with your computer you can use with yourself. For instance, if you wanted to write an essay on a friend's computer, but the friend already had a screen full of information, what would you do? Would you say forget it and go home because the screen is full? No, you would create a file and save it and call up a new file. Or you would hit the delete button.

Meanwhile, what if the computer were broken? Would you buy purple spray paint and spray it on the computer? Of course not.

How about this: Let's say we get a Nike swoosh

symbol and put it on the side of the computer. That should get it working, don't you think? No, of course not.

If that's the case, why do we think it works so well with us? Didn't we just say that the computer was just like the human brain? When we want to fix things in our lives, why do we try a new hairstyle, a new jersey or a new pair of jeans? Why don't we do the same thing we would do if we were trying to repair the computer?

We would go inside and tamper with the wires of the computer. That means we should go inside and fix our own faulty wires. We should repair our thinking. When we have bad habits we want to get rid of, ways or attitudes we don't like, we can push them out of the computer called our brain by changing the program.

Just like we change the program in the computer, we can change the program in our mind. How do we do that? By trying the same thing we tried in chapter one. We take a strong new thought called an affirmation and repeat it at least 25 times a day. That powerful thought can then become the new program in the computer called our brain. It can become the new information on our brains' computer screen. What's more, it can do something for us that our big wrestler friend couldn't accomplish.

It can make us the life of the party!

Video Exercises

1. Sit at your computer and call up a new document. Think about something negative you might have said to yourself. It could be something like "I'm not smart enough" or "I'm not good enough." Be honest about what it is you are really thinking, and then type it three times. After you type it in, read it, then delete it. You now have a blank screen to do anything you want. Think of the blank screen as your mind. Now type "I am intelligent." or "I believe in me. I am powerful, and I am strong." Type it three times. Now print it out on paper and put it on your bedroom wall. Also, try saving it in the computer and calling it up just to read sometimes. By deleting the bad message and typing in a positive one, you have just used the computer just like you would your brain.

2. If you had a chance to create your video game, what would it be? Try it. Come up with your own characters, decide how they look, how they are dressed, etc. Now come up with a theme. Are the characters racing one another or is one character chasing the other? Are they playing a game or engaged in battle? Give your video game a title and describe it in detail. When you finish, read it over and ask yourself who's in control. Do the characters have power or do you have the power? Are you making decisions or will the characters make decisions? What about your life. Do all the characters around you have the power or do you? Are you making decisions to go to the school, to study, to get angry or do the people around you push all the control buttons?

CHAPTER FIVE

THE HARDER YOU BOUNCE THE BALL, THE HIGHER IT RISES

There's a whole lot of action on the basketball court! Cheerleaders are jumping, whistles are shrieking, fans in the bleachers are stomping, shouting, and screaming at the top of their lungs.

Then, just when it seems like it can't get any more exciting, something out of the ordinary happens. A player sneaks up on a member of the opposing team and lunges for the ball. He grabs it, rushes down the court, and then bounces it so hard that it rises, rises, rises to a level several inches above the net. At that height and with that much intensity, the ball seems out of control. But it isn't.

It drops through the basketball hoop with ease.
The crowd goes wild. The winning school is chanting, yelling and dancing in their seats. It was an unusual move

and they don't know how their player managed it. He didn't slam-dunk. He didn't make a basket by tossing it from a certain angle in the auditorium.

Instead, he accomplished the unexpected. His whirling ball spun in the direction of the basket and fell in. He made it because of luck and determination. And because he understood a very basic scientific law: The harder you bounce the ball, the higher it rises.

The same principle applies to you. Whaaattt??? Are you reading this correctly? Is this chapter actually suggesting that you compare yourself to a rubber ball? The answer is yes. . . sort of. You actually can think of yourself as a round object tumbling across the court. The secret lies in how much of a push you give the ball (which in this case is you). The secret lies in how much force you apply when you bounce the ball (which, of course, is you).

You see, balls don't bounce on their own. And, neither do you. You have to exert effort. You have to go to class and listen, even when you don't feel like it. You have to study, even when it seems like drudgery. You have to do homework, complete assignments and take exams.

To meet these goals you must develop will power. In addition, you must use that will power in the right way. For instance, if one of your favorite programs is on TV but you have to take a test the following morning, it would be real tempting to reach for the remote then tell yourself you can pass without preparing. It would be real tempting to skim through the lessons quickly instead of reading them. It would be tempting to try and cheat.

But that would be the easy way out. That's letting the ball roll instead of making it bounce. When you do that,things don't go quite as well. You might find yourself failing in school or falling behind in certain classes. You might be creating a reputation that could come back to haunt you in the future, especially if you hope to one day find a good job.

The reputation you build now is the reputation that follows you later. That reputation is being affected by your willingness to take control and put some bounce into your life. Or, by your decision to just be lazy.

Often, when you face tough challenges you accomplish a lot more because you feel as if you are being pushed. That works in school, at home and with other aspects of everyday life. Let's say, for example, that you're dealing with a lot of problems with your family. It's not unusual for children to have parents who aren't getting along or happen to be going through a divorce. There are times when small troubles in the household escalate into bigger troubles: A parent starts drinking or becoming abusive.

Situations like that are messed up. But, they don't have to lead to destruction. Remember, heartaches and difficulties are like a driving force in our lives. They can be just like a ball that's thrown to the ground with a tremendous rush of energy. When that happens, the ball has power. And so it is with tough times. Those experiences can be the push we need to change a bad attitude or start setting goals.

You've heard the old expression "When the going gets tough, the tough get going." That has a powerful meaning. It suggests that without the problems, we might not try so hard. We might not push ourselves. We might not apply a lot of effort. We might not rise and rise and rise like the ball at the beginning of this chapter.

Get the picture? Maybe you aren't living with your

parents or you do live them and they simply don't spend enough time with you. Maybe you have parents who love you a lot but you feel they are too strict. You could have a little brother or sister acting like a pest. You may have boyfriend or girlfriend problems. Some people at school are making fun of you. You just got dumped, and you're hurting so much you don't know how you're going to make it through the week.

First of all, you must feel whatever emotions you are feeling. Don't block them. Express them. Share them with a friend, an older relative or a counselor at school. Give yourself time to grieve. Then take your feelings of sadness and pain and pour them into something you enjoy.

Start writing poetry or learn to play a musical instrument. Try out for sports or get involved in another extracurricular activity. Find a job, volunteer at a community center or get involved in activities at church. Decide what your talent is and spend a lot of time developing it and allowing it to grow. Think of your problem as a bouncing ball, adding the force that will lead to positive change in your life.

Does this sound unbelievable? Does it seem ridiculous to think that a problem could ever result in anything good? Well, look at it this way: Problems inspire people to achieve. Problems help people become creative. Problems encourage us to dream.

Without the problem of stuttering, actor James Earl Jones (the voice of Darth Vader in *Star Wars*) wouldn't have worked so hard to perfect his speech. And, if he hadn't worked so hard on his speech patterns, he wouldn't have developed the tremendous voice that made him famous. The same thing applies to popular funnyman,

Steve Martin (the co-star of *Bringing down the House*). As a child, he relied on silliness, laughter and jokes to cope with a dad who physically abused him. Instead of lashing out, he turned to comedy and used it to calm his anger. Likewise, if Olympic runner Wilma Rudolph hadn't had a physical disability as a child, she might not have challenged herself to become one of the world's fastest runners.

When you're trying to deal with obstacles, sometimes you bounce so hard and so high that you surprise yourself by how much you have accomplished. Other times, you give up. Like a useless, old basketball, you just sit there.

But that's breaking the rules of the game! The basketball is supposed to keep bouncing, isn't it? The ball is expected to hit the ground a few times. When it does, it builds up power and speed.

Think about that the next time you feel like you have hit rock bottom. The circumstances that make us feel low are often the circumstances that encourage us to aim higher. The harder the times are now, the better things might be later. The tougher life is now, the happier it can become in the years ahead.

Of course, that only works when we believe the struggles in our lives aren't meant to destroy us. They are meant to make us strong. They are meant to prepare us for something BRIGHTER, BETTER and far more BEAUTIFUL.

Problem Solving Exercises

The Journey of the Moth

There's an old tale about a curious man who happened to spot a cocoon in his backyard. We all know what cocoons are. They are spun by caterpillars that are transforming into moths. Well, evidently this caterpillar had completed the transformation process. There was a small hole at the end of the cocoon and the man could see the spindly legs of a moth, struggling to get out. The man was excited because he had never witnessed a moth emerging from a cocoon. So he stopped and waited. But it was taking an awfully long time. The caterpillar-turned-moth was struggling so hard and having such a tough time the man decided to help it out. He began tearing the opening and making it bigger, large enough for the creature to fly out with ease. When he finished, that didn't happen. Rather than fly, the moth fell to the ground. The man's heartbeat quickened and he hung around for he felt certain the insect would be flapping its wings at any moment. He waited and waited. Ten, maybe twenty minutes passed and all the butterfly did was wiggle. Finally, after wiggling for the last time, it curled up and died. The man was so upset he rushed to the library and checked out a book on moths and butterflies. He wanted to find out what had gone wrong. This is what he discovered: When the newly formed moth is emerging from the cocoon, it must squeeze its body through a tiny opening. As it squeezes through, its fragile wings press against the edges of the cocoon and that pressure causes the blood vessels of the wings to fill up with blood and grow beautiful, sturdy and strong.

1. The man made the process too easy. In his attempt to be helpful, he eliminated the struggle. In doing so, he prevented the moth from developing the strength to survive. What is the moral of this story?

2. How would you apply the moth story to your life?

3. You say you have problems. Try this: Think about yourself gripping a basketball. Now, hold that image in your head. Picture yourself slamming it down like the player who landed the winning point for his team. Write a description of how it feels. Next, picture yourself dealing with a difficulty in your life and bouncing back. Write a description of how you overcame the problem and how it made you feel. Remember, be positive!

4. The sun doesn't shine all the time. Sometimes, it has to rain. Does that expression have personal meaning in your life? Why is the rain as important as the sunshine? (For example, the sun helps flowers grow, but flowers also need rain). Why are the challenges of school and/or your personal life as important as the fun times?

5. After the rainbow, comes the rain. Give an example of rain in your life turning into a rainbow. If it hasn't happened, how can you help create a rainbow?

CHAPTER SIX
STOP HATING & START PLAYING

It has happened so many times, you probably can't keep track You're in class or standing in the hallway at school when someone makes a crack about the way you look or the way you dress. Maybe the person is joking. Maybe he isn't. Either way, you don't like being put on the spot like that and you don't understand why it's happening.

So what exactly is going on?

(A.) This person is an enemy who's going out of the way to try and make you look bad.

(B.) The person has an anger management problem.

(C.) This is a clear case of player hating.

The answer is all of the above. The green-eyed monster known as jealousy has surfaced and when that happens, things can get pretty ugly.

But it does happen. No matter who you are, you're going to experience the effects of jealousy now and then. Sometimes, you're the victim — the person being envied and talked about. Other times, you might even be the person doing the damage. That's right, there may come a time when you actually feel pangs of jealousy toward someone else.

There's a solution. When you're the target of someone's envy, try to focus on yourself rather than placing your focus on his or her actions. People who are jealous are in pain. They have been trying to achieve a goal that you have achieved or to capture a certain look that seems to come naturally to you. Whatever it is, they can't seem to accomplish it, and they can't handle the failure.

No one has taught them the lessons you are about to learn. And that is simply, you handle life better when you stop comparing yourself to others. Of course, that's easier said than done. It's really easy for us to say we're not going to compare ourselves to someone else. But, when it comes to the way we react to what's going on — in school, after school when we're dealing with friends and even with the way we dress — comparison is the method most of us rely on.

Why? We haven't been taught anything else. Most of us have been conditioned to believe that we are successful when we come in number one in a race, when we come in number one on an exam, when we come in number one in a dance contest or athletic competition.

Unfortunately, we are so used to comparing that we allow it to define who we are. However, there are much more effective and positive ways for learning to appreciate our true talents and our own unique qualities.

You see, a person who always compares herself or himself to others will always feel bad because there will always be someone smarter, more attractive or a better dresser. If you want to feel good about you, you have to stop looking around. Instead, you have to look within.

In other words, stop hating and start playing. When you're checking everybody else out, you're worrying. When you're checking out yourself, you're playing and you're winning in the game of life. When you're checking yourself out, you're admiring yourself and giving yourself a daily dose of strong compliments. You're doing affirmations and learning to pat yourself on the back.

When you're checking yourself out, pumping yourself up and telling yourself positive things, your true power kicks in. You're not concerned about what person X is saying or what person Y is wearing. You're focusing on the person who is with you 365 days a year. That's you! And only *you* have power over what *you* think and feel.

You exercise that power when you decide to stop measuring yourself according to standards set by others. Others may succeed. Others may fail. That is their personal path in life, their individual journey. What they accomplish has nothing to do with you. What you achieve has nothing to do with them.

You can create your own personal set of standards based on your ideals and expectations. For instance, let's just say you are tall and dark. In your case, tall and dark should be considered wonderful traits that make you feel proud and confident.

If you are pale, or freckled, short or full-figured, feel good about those physical characteristics as well. WHO SAYS THEY ARE NOT POSITIVE? Your peers? Your brother or sister? Certain recording artists? Characters on TV? Well, PROVE THEM WRONG!!! Take a stand by making powerful statements to yourself about yourself, no matter what the critics say. Refuse to let others dictate to you how you should look, what you should buy, what you should wear. It's up to you to call the shots. You are the mayor, governor and president of your own thoughts.

Get Behind The Wheel Of Your Mind.

If you are going to control those thoughts, you have to get behind the wheel of your own mind and steer. What's more, you are going to have to learn how to be as skilled and determined as a champion race car driver, twisting around curves, revving up the engine and speeding toward the finish line.

You can't win if you're craning your neck trying to see what another driver in another car is doing. You can't and won't win if you're fussing with your outfit and wondering if it's as cool as the one the person in the next car is wearing. You're sure to lose if your mind is on anything but the race. The key words here are simple:

Pay Attention To Yourself.

If you're roaring down a race track at 300 mph, you have to be in control. Multi-millionaire, motivational speaker Anthony Robbins believes the ups and downs of everyday life challenge us in the same way. When we're moving ahead in either life or a race, we're zooming. Our adrenalin is flowing, our hearts are beating furiously.

At a time like that, we can't afford to get lost in thought about things that don't matter, can we? The only thing that matters is that we keep our eyes on our own private road. That means your road. That means your lane. That means your car.

Robbins, who once took up race car driving as a sport, says he learned valuable lessons about getting ahead while he was whizzing around the track. But the most important lesson is one he still lives by to this day.

DON'T LOOK AT THE WALL!!!!!.

Why not? Race car drivers moving at unbelievable speed are bound to lose control of the car sometimes. When that happens, they are told not to look at the wall. If they look at the wall, they will run into it. They cannot allow their minds to wander away from the track.

To this day, Robbins uses that bit of advice when problems, setbacks and difficult people happen to stumble onto his path. They are the wall, just like negative friends, loud-talking schoolmates and classes that you think you can't pass. The wall is anything that looms in front of you and makes you feel as if you are going to crash.

You avoid crashing when you look at all the wonderful possibilities that lay ahead. Certain friends will insist that you take detours. People who want to see you fail will try and cause accidents. They are the wall. Ignore them. Put your pedal to the metal, as they say, and keep driving toward your goal.

Pause only for stop signs and stoplights. (Those are parents and teachers). Slow down, listen, then cruise on. Remember, maneuver past anyone who acts as a speed bump or tries to lead you down rocky and dangerous paths.

This is your own personal adventure. Stick with it and, soon, you will learn to develop your special talents and celebrate your unique gifts. Before long, you won't even notice the player haters. (You'll even drop the word "hate" from your vocabulary.) Before long, you'll be setting goals, making plans and heading toward success.

Congratulations! You are on your way!

Steering Exercises

1. Make a list of important personal qualities. Do not describe the way you look. Include talents, skills and personality traits only.

2. Think about a person at school or challenge in your life that is bothering you. Write it down. Next, write down something pleasant you could focus on whenever that person or that challenge comes to mind. Be as positive as you can.

3. Everybody doesn't get everything, but we all get something. Whatever it is, take pride in it and develop it. Don't let it wither away while you waste precious time trying to imitate someone else. Learn to count your blessings and learn to take the bitter with the sweet. Start now by making a list of all the things you have to be grateful for. Is it your parents? On the other hand, you might have the kind of family that's not in your corner. But then again you could have a favorite aunt or an uncle who showers you with love. Can you sing or play an instrument? When you run, are you the fastest kid on the track? Make sure you include opportunities and positive experiences on your list (concerts or trips out of town).
When you're feeling down, pick up the list. There, in black and white, will be a stark reminder that things aren't so bad. As you read it, you will feel the need to pay attention to what *you* have, rather than worry about what someone else supposedly is getting.

CHAPTER SEVEN

DON'T BE A PARTY CRASHER

That does it!
Boy, that person was soooo wrong. It's enough to make you start swinging. You're so mad you can't even think straight. It's like you've been blinded. You're boiling with anger. You're burning up inside. You're so upset, you see stars. And, before long, (gulp) you're plotting revenge.

STOP RIGHT THERE! Hold it a minute. Before you go any further, get a grip on yourself. Wait. Count to ten. Think. Take a deep, deep breath. Listen to the soft voice (those words of reason) within.

You're not behaving responsibly when you let anger rush into your mind like a burglar and kick in the doors that lead to your common sense. But when you get upset, that's what happens sometimes. Your thoughts become stormy and you get caught up in getting back at the person who harmed you. You feel injured. As a result, you start saying things you probably shouldn't say, or walking around feeling sad, disgusted, and even depressed.

After awhile, you get so down and out that you officially become a party crasher. Don't get this wrong; you're not messing up anyone else's party. You're not showing up uninvited and screwing up someone else's good time.

You're affecting yourself. You're ruining your own feelings of peace, your own joy and your own excitement. It's probably true: that other person might have been a jerk. That friend, enemy, adult, or child, might have caused you incredible pain. But here's a secret. When something is over, it is over. And when it is over, it cannot harm you anymore — unless you let it.

You allow it to continue to harm you when you continue to think about it. When you dwell on it, you pull off the bandage and pick at the wound. When you pick at the wound, it stings all over again.

Yet that's what some of us do. Some of us hang on to sour memories and relive the difficult times. But why dwell on a bad thing that another individual did to you? Why let all those reckless thoughts stomp around your own brain, crashing your own party?

Yes, believe it or not, there is a party going on in your head at times. When you're laughing, singing, watching a great movie or talking on the phone to your best friend, the pictures flickering in your mind are bright, positive and happy. They start fading when you get mad. When you cling to the anger, they curl up and die.

For instance, what if a so-called friend is taking you through a lot of drama. This person (who is really only pretending to be your friend) may have made up lies about you or gossiped behind your back. When situations like that occur, you get all fired up and, unfortunately, you suffer.

All the good thoughts in your mind are suffocated — drowned out by a river of painful emotions. You know the feeling. It's almost like you're woozy, right?

There's only one way to get yourself back on track and get the party going again. You have to FORGIVE.

Forgiveness isn't as weak and wimpy as some people think. Many people believe that when you forgive someone, you let them off the hook. They think people who forgive are allowing themselves to be smacked down. Or that they are cowards.

Actually, it's the other way around. People who forgive are strong. People who forgive are making a decision to let go of the pain churning inside their spirits and to allow their hearts to return to a state of celebration. People forgive because they want to feel better. People forgive because they don't want to become party crashers in their own lives.

When anger is sloshing around in your mind, it makes you miserable. You make bad choices. You're frustrated. In fact, the friend, associate or enemy who may have caused you pain is feeling a whole lot better than you're feeling — sleeping with your anger.

They have experienced a victory. If you think you are getting back at them by hating them, talking about them, or plotting revenge, think again. There is only one way to get even. You have to get happy. You have to promise yourself that no one can anger you enough to rob you of your joy.

Pretend you are holding a contract that was put

together by a lawyer. Pretend you are in the lawyer's office, signing the contract and preparing to give it to the person who hurt you. Before you hand it over, pause and read these important words:

"When you sign this document, you will have the power to make me miserable forever."

Would you sign it? If you're still angry, you wouldn't have to. As long as you're seething inside, you don't need a contract to give your enemy permission to make you feel bad. It's already happening.

Now, picture yourself laughing and taking the document back. Picture yourself tearing it up in front of the person's face. By forgiving them, you are taking control of your own emotions. When you forgive them, they can no longer haunt you. They can't get anywhere near your heart. The chains are broken now. You are free.

Yes, they were wrong. Yes, you were right. But do you want to be right? Or do you want to be happy? Do you want to have a good time? Or do you want to be a party crasher in your own mind?

Forgiveness Exercises

1. Make a list of all the people you need to forgive. Next to each person's name, write: "I forgive you."

2. Think of someone who has hurt you in some way. Write the person's name down. Next to his or her name, write a statement explaining why their actions made you feel bad. Once again, write: "I forgive you."

3. Look at each name on the list above. Do you know anything about the personal background or past experiences of these individuals? If you do, write a sentence about what may have caused them to behave the way they do. If you don't know anything about them, write this statement: "I don't know what makes you behave the way you do. Rather than judge you, I will think thoughts of peace."

4. Do you feel angry when you think about certain people or circumstances? Write down the names of the individuals or the specifics about the circumstances. Next, write these words: "I release you. I am taking my power back. I forgive you and I am free."

5. Repeat exercise four. Next to each name or circumstance, write "I would rather be happy."

6. Write letters or notes of forgiveness to the individuals on your list. Put them in helium-filled balloons and release them.

7. Are there people or situations that make you feel happy whenever you think about them? Write those down. Whenever you think about the things that make you angry, immediately switch your mind to thoughts that make you feel good.

8. Think about a person or circumstance that made you angry. Now think about a happy experience. Picture yourself either at a basketball game or having fun at a dance or riding an amusement park ride. Hold on to that image. At least three times a week, practice flashing it in you mind over and over again. Next time someone upsets you, quickly conjure it up.

9. Think about the experience that upset you. Can you picture it? Good. Now take the pictures in your mind and move them in reverse. Does that make you laugh? Now make the picture smaller and smaller in your mind so that it seems far away. Try this every now and then. It works!

10. Remember to say daily affirmations. Try these:
A. I forgive ....(write in person's name)
B. I totally forgive everyone.
C. I am a forgiving person. Forgiveness is cool.
D. I forgive. I am free.

CHAPTER EIGHT
WHEN LOVE CALLS

In the old days, street corner entertainers with shiny, slick hair-dos' hung around lamp posts for hours singing about their undying passion for someone who dumped them and gave them the blues. They'd do anything, or so the songs said, to get their loved ones back. As they put it, they even had to "go outside in the rain," to hide the tears (because they were crying just that much).

Today, ballads aren't so ridiculously sentimental and the lyrics aren't quite as syrupy. Artists aren't harmonizing about heavenly relationships as much or claiming they won't go on living if someone kicks them to the curb. But if you're attending a modern high school or middle school, you know that the invisible melody of love is still making its presence known. It's in the air. It's in the hallways. It's in the swagger of the boys, the giggles of girls. It's in the chatter, the tough talk, the notes passed around in class.

You and your friends probably have love on your minds. And sometimes, it can get pretty intense. Some of you approach love with a seriousness and as a form of possession. Many of you cling to relationships and they become part of your identity.

Love pounds in your heart, floods your minds and, at times, prevents you from thinking of anything else. Love gives you a sense of being grown-up and fills you with the desire to tackle responsibilities you're not ready to handle.

In fact, it's time for a reality check: No one can honestly assess what you're feeling but you. Yet, odds are, it's not true love unless you're extremely mature and possess an enormous amount of self-love. Why? Only a teen who loves himself or herself is capable of sincerely loving another.

Sure, you might think you're in love. No doubt you think about him or her all the time. No doubt there is a yearning, accompanied by an intense need. It's the real thing; it has to be. What else could explain the frustration you feel when that significant person doesn't call or when, dare we say it, you see him or her talking to someone else?

No, he didn't just look at another girl and wink! No, she didn't just give her phone number to another guy! It's enough to make you jump right out of your skin. That's love you're feeling, isn't it? That's love because it's the only time you have ever behaved this way. Your heart's thumping and you don't know what you're going to do.

Well, hold on. Real love is not a burning feeling. It is concern as in wanting the best for another human being. How can we claim to want the best for someone else when many of us don't even know how to claim the best for ourselves.

When we want the best for ourselves, we demand respect. A guy treats a girl with a respect. The same treatment is expected of her in return. But a girl who doesn't really care about herself will allow a guy to talk to her in any manner, however embarrassing. A guy who doesn't yet recognize his self-worth will let a young lady use him.

Before either of them can truly understand how to love another, they must first understand what it means to love oneself. What is love of the self? It's caring for perhaps the greatest concern in your life right now. That's you! It's learning to take care of you. It's understanding that if you're pushing your own needs aside constantly to cater to someone else you're not loving that person, you're simply doing what you can to win his or her affection. You're not loving that person because you're not loving yourself.

Love of self is a tricky challenge. Many people, teens and adults alike, think they love themselves because they drape their bodies in the best of clothing. They think they have a high self-esteem because they curse out people who have disrespected them. They think they are shining examples of self-confidence because they seek out and demand attention. And when things don't go their way, they make a scene.

That's not self-love. That's insecurity! Only insecure individuals need constant attention. Only a person who is insecure needs to build himself or herself up by publicly humiliating someone else. And clothing, although a sign of good grooming, personal style and taste, doesn't always indicate that you value who you are.

Some people buy a lot of clothes because it's a way of making up for their lack of self-worth. The more clothes they own, the better they feel. They know they look good because the designer label on their jacket is a sign of what they view as the best of taste. They think they're hot because the receipt in their shopping bag says so. They feel they're attractive because their clothes are attractive. They believe they're special because the price tag hanging from their new coat declares that, "Yes, they got it going on." Why else would they or could they afford to pay so much money for a single item?

But beneath it all, sometimes lies a mind that is filled with confusion and a spirit that is using things to fill the void inside. People who recognize their value realize that jewelry and shoes are just objects they happen to have in their lives. The true measure of their worth is found in how they feel about who they are. It lies in what's going on inside of them. It lies in what is stirring in their soul.

When a person feels whole, he or she takes pride in the unique talents and the personal qualities that make him or her stand out in a crowd. That person doesn't need to look for a girl for validation. And that girl doesn't need to reach to a boy to find acceptance or to determine that she's okay.

He knows he's okay with or without her. She knows she's okay whether he is in her life or not. True self-worth comes from understanding that other people enhance our lives. They complement our lives. They add joy and support and comfort.

But they are not the main ingredient in our world. The Earth does not revolve around them. And neither should we.

So, what happens when teens who don't have this

awareness say they love one another? Control issues creep in. The boy, who wants to feel like a man, can only feel like one if his girl does what he says when he says it because he says it. If she does, then he thinks he's all right. He's down. He's the stuff.

The girl, who wants to feel loved, will try to control the boy who says he loves her. Or she'll try to possess him. Or she will allow herself to fall completely under his control. She is convinced he loves her and perceives his tendency to dominate her (even if it's abusive) as his way of showing her he cares.

Without him, she is nothing. Without her, he feels less than a man. Together, they are groping their way through a maze of confusing emotions that they have mistakenly labeled as love.

But if they back up, they can start by working on themselves. The girl can learn to believe in herself by looking in the mirror daily and telling herself "I love you." Ditto for the young man. Then, both of them can flood their minds with positive affirmations.

That's when the healing will occur. When they begin to understand that their male-female relationship is simply a reflection of the one-on-one relationship they are having with themselves, they will be making the first step toward a happy, healthy union.

Teens do love one another. You are best buddies, loyal friends, young people who understand the same music, the same language, the same joys, concerns, victories and frustrations of everyday living. But you won't be able to take that to the next level until you develop the thoughts and attitudes that lead you to a happy relationship and get rid of the ones that lead to a broken heart.

If you want love, first make a list of the things you like

about yourself and the things you don't. Read the list daily. Cherish the things you like about yourself and decide how you're going to change the things that need to be changed. Embrace yourselves before you embrace another. Then and only then will you be ready to step it up a notch. Then and only then will you be ready to enter an exciting and wonderful new phase of life. You'll be ready for the world of dating:

You'll be ready to create a healthy happy, long-lasting romance.

Relationship Exercises

1. Write down all the personal qualities you really like. Do not include physical qualities. Read this list at least once a day. (This exercise is also in chapter six.)

2. Write down the personal characteristics you would like to change, then write down your plan for improvement. What affirmation will you say or step will you take to eliminate the bad habits you do not want? (For this exercise, do not focus on physical traits.)

3. This time, jot down physical qualities that you enjoy. Your nice complexion, nice physique or nice smile.

4. Draw a line down the center of a sheet of paper. Jot down physical qualities you don't feel good about on one side. On the other side, write down something positive you can say about that characteristic you don't like. For example, if you wrote I'm overweight on one side, on the other side write the words; "I love my body just the way it is and I'm getting better all the time." If you wrote "too skinny," write down "I have the body of a fashion model." If you wrote, "too short," write "good things come in small packages." Or say "I am a powerhouse in a compact body." If you're a boy (or a girl), say "It's not the size. It's the energy, confidence and determination." If you're a girl, you might try writing: "I'm cute and petite." In other words, if you don't like a certain trait, write it down and force yourself to think of something very positive to say about it.

5. Are you in a relationship? Discuss the relationship and how well the two of you relate to each other. Do you consider it a healthy relationship? Explain why?

6. Have you ever been in a relationship that involved a lot of drama and control issues? Are you in one now? Think about the problems and ask yourself why you dealt with them or continue to deal with them. What characteristic do you need to develop to avoid patterns like this in the future? If you need to love yourself more, write that down, then discuss the tools you will use from this book and steps you will take to learn how to increase your self-love.

CHAPTER NINE
LESSONS, THAT'S WHAT'S UP

Congratulations! You made it this far and you're ready to learn even more. Okay, well let's get going. This is a quick chapter, but an important one. Read through it and study the lessons. They're designed to help you enjoy the party of life and ace the big exam (coming up next).

1. Don't take or drink anything that clouds your mind and affects your ability to make decisions. Your friends will try to convince you that it's the thing to do. It isn't. It will have a weird effect on your brain and an even weirder effect on your life.

2. Things sometimes go wrong in order to go right. The situation might seem really tough. But hang in there. One of the rules of life is that nothing ever stays exactly the same. They either get better or they get worse. Try to make the best of bad times and watch them explode into good times and great opportunities.

3. Make all experiences serve you. The challenges in your life might make you feel hopeless. But you are never helpless. It's up to you to search for a spark of joy deep inside of the problem. Could be you were turned down for the cheer team then decided to find another way to spend your time. You try out for a school play and land the lead role!

4. Life has tests. Sometimes our problems are actually tests. Other times, our friends test us. Let's say a lot of the kids at school are doing something you know they shouldn't do. You're so tempted that it hurts to resist. But no matter how much you ache you don't give in. Because of it, you're developing something called Will Power! (And you're passing the test.)

5. Things are never as bad as they seem. Your parents are busy. You don't like your stepfather. You don't feel loved. Or, you're being shuffled from relative to relative, home to home. Yet there's a grandparent, an uncle, a minister at church. There's a kind neighbor or school counselor. Someone is offering support. Pay attention to their guidance and listen when they point out your special qualities. Use this time to explore your talents, develop strength and become *determined* to be the best you can be.

6. If they make you angry, they win. A strange guy hanging around outside of your school calls you a name and makes you so mad that you jump on him. It turns out the guy doesn't attend the school. So he's not affected. But you get expelled. Who really won the fight?

7. Fake It. No, you don't believe you can do it. Try it anyway. Think positive thoughts anyway. Just Pretend. Act as if you are calm. Behave as if you are confident. Fantasize about being successful. The results will feel like magic.

8. Sorry is a five-letter word. Everyone makes mistakes sometimes, but it takes a big person to admit it. When you've done something wrong, don't waste energy hiding it, lying about it or acting as if it didn't happen. Be honest. Own up to it, apologize, then promise yourself you will do better next time. Forgiving yourself is just as important as forgiving others.

9. If you're having a party, invite the right guests. That means, be careful about the company you keep. It really is true about birds of a feather flocking together. Or as another common expression says: "If you hang around with dogs, you'll get fleas." Don't deal with your anger by surrounding yourself with other kids just as frustrated as you are. Find positive solutions to your troubles and seek out friends who lift you up rather than those who pull you down.

10. Consider the Consequences. For every action there is a reaction. If you do something major like smoking weed or shoplifting, the consequences are major, i.e. going to court, facing a judge and ending up in jail. If you do something that seems minor like ignoring a homework assignment or staying up so late you can't make it on time for school, the consequences might not get you expelled or in trouble with the law, but you will have to deal with something unpleasant. As a result of your behavior, you might not do well in school or worse you might not graduate. When everything is said and done, you'll only have one person to blame. YOU.

11. Tell the Truth.

Many people think lies are harmless. They are not! When you don't tell the truth, friends and family members stop trusting you. What's worse, others are seriously affected. Reputations are damaged. Jobs are lost. Lives are ruined. In some instances, you end up telling a second or third lie just to support the first lie. Throughout it all, you lose respect for someone very important — yourself. (For help with this lesson, look for the truth affirmation in chapter 3.)

12. Keep Your Promises.

No one likes a hypocrite. If you want people to take you seriously, become a person of your word. Don't agree to do things you have no intention of doing. Don't agree with statements and ideas that don't reflect your core beliefs. In other words, be honest with yourself.

Review

1. Which lesson means the most to you? Explain why.

2. Pick one lesson and figure out how it applies to your life. Discuss your feelings with friends.

3. Write about an incident in your life that taught you one of the lessons. Which lesson is it?

4. Can you think of a time when you pretended you were confident or feeling positive but you really felt scared? How did it feel to pretend? Did it work? Write about your experience.

5. Have you ever felt like lying and decided it was best to tell the truth. What were the consequences? Are you glad you chose honesty over dishonesty?

CHAPTER TEN

THE BIG EXAM !

So we said life's a party. Well, what about the exams? Get ready. They're coming. This one is just the beginning.

1. What are affirmations?

A. Original ideas

B. Compliments you give to other people

C. A positive statement you make to yourself about yourself.

D. A positive statement you share with someone else.

2. What's so bad about comparing yourself to someone else?

A. Comparing yourself to others makes you jealous of them.

B. Comparing yourself to others is conceited.

D. Comparison is time consuming.

E. There's always someone more attractive or smarter. It's best to focus on your own unique talents and gifts.

3. Why are thoughts like dollar bills?

A. Money is the only thing as powerful as thoughts.

B. Thoughts are like dollar bills because thinking about something is just like buying it or making an investment in it.

C. Thoughts are green just like dollar bills.

D. Thoughts aren't like dollars. That was just a joke.

4. Is it possible to fake your way into accomplishing a goal?

A. Yes, you fake something by pretending it until you believe it.

B. You can't fake a goal. You either have it or you don't.

C. Never fake it. That's not being honest with yourself.

D. Faking is for losers.

5. What does it mean to give your power away?

A. Giving your power away means not fighting back when people put you down.

B. When you cry at any time, you have given your power away.

C. You give away power when you allow society and/or other people to tell you what you should believe and how you should feel about yourself.

D. You give away power when you don't talk back to your teacher.

6. How do you take your power back?

A. Fighting.

B. Making sure you're strapped.

C. Cursing out anyone who talks about you.

D. Saying daily affirmations to build character and inner strength.

7. Why did the moth die when a man in the park helped it out of the cocoon?
A. Moths should never come in contact with humans.
B. The man's hands were dirty.
C. The moth needed the struggle and pressure of slowly squeezing out of the cocoon because that experience would have helped it build strong wings.
D. The man let the moth out too soon.

8. How often should one say affirmations?
A. Three times a day
B. Once a week
C. Once a day
D. At least 25 times a day

9. Are problems a terrible curse that one should avoid at all times?
A. Yes, problems are a sign that your life will never improve.
B. No, problems can help you develop strength. They can also lead to opportunities.
C. Yes, avoid problems because they are a sign that you don't have your life together.
D. Problems are negative because they bring you down.

10. When you're unhappy, what can you do to make yourself feel better?
A. Criticize someone else.
B. Tell jokes about your little brother or sister.
C. Talk on the phone.
D. Think about a happy situation.

11. Is it possible to feel good when you're dealing with a lot of problems?

A. No, problems are depressing.

B. No, you don't have anything to be happy about.

C. Yes, you have the power to change your mood by thinking about the good things in your life.

D. No, if you pretend you're feeling good when you're not, you're not facing reality.

12. Why are thoughts powerful?

A. They can make you happy or sad.

B. Your thoughts are like magnets that can attract happy or negative experiences.

C. Thoughts aren't powerful. That's just an expression.

D. You have no control over them. They are meaningless.

13. What's the best way to develop self control?

A. Say an affirmation whenever something goes wrong.

B. Sing your favorite song.

C. Pick on someone you don't like.

D. Say positive affirmations every single day.

14. What happens when you don't take charge of your own thoughts?

A. You start imagining things.

B. The media, other people, song lyrics, bad memories and other negative influences sometimes take control.

C. You have a boring life.

D. People talk about you.

15. Do affirmations build self-confidence?
A. No. Affirmations help build careers in science.
B. Affirmations only help when you already have confidence and a good attitude.
C. Affirmations are a positive way for anyone to develop self-confidence and learn to believe in their dreams and goals.
D. Affirmations are for rap artists only.

16. How did Michael Jordan develop the skills that made him a superstar?
A. He bought an expensive new basketball.
B. He practiced whenever he felt like it.
C. He wore the best brand of athletic shoes.
D. He practiced a lot, set goals and constantly pictured himself slam-dunking the ball.

17. Write down at least three affirmations from the first chapter, then make up one of your own. (Make sure your affirmation is written in the present tense.)
A.
B.
C.
D.

18. Which statement is an example of a true affirmation?
A. I think life will get better if I apply myself.
B. I am enjoying a wonderful life.
C. Life sucks!
D. I am going to try and maybe things will eventually change.

19. If you're feeling bad about yourself, should you just put yourself down if that's what you're feeling?

A. Of course, since that's how you feel.

B. Yes, putting yourself down is a way of facing things as they are.

C. No. Positive thoughts are the best way to improve your attitude and your life.

D. When you feel bad, acting positive only makes you feel worse.

20. If someone at school is saying negative things about you, does that mean you, how should you respond?

A. Jump them after school.

B. Tell them what you think of their behavior.

C. Say positive affirmations to yourself over and over again every day.

D. Tell the person who's talking about you to say affirmations.

21. If you're having a tough life, should you say things like "my life is horrible?"

A. Yes, if your life is bad, you should go on and admit it.

B. Yes, you're telling the truth, and truth is positive.

C. No, saying bad things won't make it better. You should say your life is good in order to help to improve it.

D. Never lie to yourself about how bad your life is.

22. If you're not doing well in school, can an affirmation help you improve study habits?

A. Yes. When repeated daily, affirmations can help improve any area of your life.

B. No. Affirmations only apply to money and career goals.

C. No, because affirmations are just statements. They don't have anything to do with schoolwork.

D. No way! Affirmations are for people who already have it going on.

23. A writer named Emmet Fox compared affirmations to nails. Why?

A. The sharpness of nails reminds him of affirmations.

B. A carpenter pushes an old nail out by hammering a new nail in the same way that old thoughts are pushed out by positive new affirmation thoughts.

C. Affirmations are like hammers and nails represent the human brain.

D. Affirmations are positive work and nails are the positive work of a carpenter.

24. What should you do when someone acts jealous of you?

A. Tell them off.

B. Gossip about them.

C. Tell them they're not perfect either and give them a list of affirmations to do.

D. Focus on yourself and pump yourself up by saying positive things.

25. If you have tried to be positive and things are still going wrong, should you give up?

A. Yes, positive thoughts should work within a few months. Besides, people are laughing at you.

B. Give up because you're just wasting time and making yourself feel silly.

C. Never give up no matter what. Keep saying affirmations over and over until you finally believe them.

D. Give up. Not everyone can be positive.

26. A friend is trying to talk you into taking drugs? How could an affirmation help you with that problem?

A. This is one thing that even affirmations can't help.

B. The person who is tempting you will get scared if he or she finds out you're saying affirmations.

C. Affirmations are so powerful you will feel too strong and positive to let anyone talk you into anything you don't want to do.

D. When you say affirmations, drugs don't work.

27. If you're already positive and happy with yourself the way you are, why should you be concerned about affirmations?

A. No matter how positive you are, you can always become more positive to prepare yourself for the possible challenges of the future.

B. You don't need affirmations. Ignore them.

C. Don't say affirmations. Your life is always going to be perfect.

D. You'll become negative if you don't.

28. How can positive thinking help when someone is dealing with decisions about sex or getting out of an abusive relationship?

A. When you're thinking positive, a bad relationship doesn't bother you that much.

B. When you're a positive person, you're not interested in the opposite sex.

C. Positive thoughts don't make a difference in this case.

D. When a person's mind is filled with positive thoughts, that person is stronger and filled with self-respect. As a result, he or she will not tolerate a relationship that makes them feel unworthy. They also are more prone to make responsible decisions about their bodies and their sexuality.

29. Why is it important to forgive?
A. If you don't forgive someone who caused you pain, they might come back and start more trouble.
B. It's important to forgive because you release yourself from the misery of anger. Holding grudges causes pain to the person who holds the grudge. When you forgive, you set yourself free.
C. You should forgive because there are new stores at the mall that pass out free ice cream to people who forgive others.
D. Actually, it's best not to forgive. If you do, the person who harmed you will never understand how much you are suffering.

30. If you're feeling confused and angry, what should you do?
A. Seek revenge on the person who made you angry.
B. Scream and shout at everyone in your home.
C. Stop focusing on the things that are all wrong and start setting goals, talking to counselors and concentrating on ways to make your life better.
D. Hang around with other people who are angry and looking for trouble.

If you've finished the test, you're probably eager to fast forward to the results. For those who have permission, check out the answers on the final page. For those who don't, wait and get results from an instructor.

Remember, this is just one exam out of many you'll be taking through the years. But if you pay attention to the rules, they'll get easier and easier. So, don't worry. Just learn as you go along. And have fun.

WELCOME TO THE PARTY OF LIFE!

Exam Answers

1. C 2. E

3. B 4. A

5. C 6. D

7. C 8. D

9. B 10. D

11. C 12. B

13. D 14. B

15. C 16. D

17. No answer 18. B

19. C 20. C

21. C 22. A

23. B 24. D

25. C 26. C

27. A 28. D

29. B 30. C

ABOUT THE AUTHOR

A veteran journalist, Denise Crittendon is the founding editor of *African American Family Magazine* in Ferndale, Mich. and the first woman to be appointed editor of *The Crisis*, the official publication of the NAACP. Her true passion is motivating youth to be all that they can be. She speaks to young women and men at churches, schools and community centers and encourages them to reach deep within to realize their true power, strength and tenacity. She was honored with a Spirit of Detroit Award and the Life Direction's Mary Ball Children's Advocacy Award for her first book, *Girl In The Mirror, A Teen's Guide To Self Awareness*. It was recognized by *Essence* and highly recommended by *The Detroit News, The Detroit Free Press, The Michigan Chronicle, The Michigan Citizen*, RawSistaz.com and more. In *Life Is A Party*, Ms.Crittendon uses music, video game imagery and sports to lead teens on an exciting journey into self fulfillment, dignity and empowerment.

To order copies of

Life Is A Party That Comes With Exams

and/or

Girl In the Mirror, A Teen's Guide To Self-Awareness :

Visit - www.esteemmultimedia.com

Or send check or money order to:

Esteem Multi Media
200 Riverfront Drive #8j, Detroit, MI 48226

Life Is A Party That Comes With Exams @ $12.95
Girl in the Mirror, A Teen's Guide To Self-Awareness @ $12.95
Shipping and handling $2.00: $1.00 each additional book

"WHEN YOU PUT YOUR MIND TO IT,
ANYTHING CAN HAPPEN."

-from the Karate Kid